HOW DO I
DEAL
WITH
DIFFICULT
PEOPLE?

BRYAN LARSON

**SMITH
FREEMAN
Publishing**

How Do I Deal with Dificult People?

Bible verses were taken from the following translations:

KJV: The Holy Bible, King James Version

HCSB: Scripture quotations marked HCSB®, are taken from the Holman Christian Standard Bible®, Copyright © 1999, 2000, 2002, 2003, 2009 by Holman Bible Publishers. Used by permission. HCSB® is a federally registered trademark of Holman Bible Publishers.

MSG: Scriptures marked MSG are taken from the THE MESSAGE: THE BIBLE IN CONTEMPORARY ENGLISH (MSG), copyright©1993, 1994, 1995, 1996, 2000, 2001, 2002. Used by permission of NavPress Publishing Group.

NASB: Scripture quotations taken from the New American Standard Bible®, Copyright © 1960, 1962, 1963, 1968, 1971, 1972, 1973, 1975, 1977, 1995 by The Lockman Foundation. Used by permission.

NCV: Scripture taken from the New Century Version. Copyright © 1987, 1988, 1991 by Thomas Nelson, Inc. Used by permission. All rights reserved.

NIV: Scripture quotations marked (NIV) are taken from The Holy Bible, New International Version® NIV®. copyright © 1973, 1978, 1984, 2011 by Biblica, Inc.™ Used by permission of Zondervan. All rights reserved worldwide. www.zondervan.com. "NIV" and "New International Version" are trademarks registered in the United States patent and trademark office by Biblica, Inc.™

NKJV: Scripture taken from the New King James Version. Copyright © 1982 by Thomas Nelson, Inc. Used by permission. All rights reserved.

NLT: Holy Bible, New Living Translation, copyright © 1996, 2004, 2007, 2015 by Tyndale House Foundation. Used by permission of Tyndale House Publishers, Inc. All rights reserved.

ISBN: 978-0-9986529-8-6

ABOUT THE AUTHOR

Bryan Larson is a seasoned leader, a gifted coach, and a sought-after teacher who has spent the last nineteen years strengthening ministries around the globe. Known for his boundless energy, peerless insight, and deep conviction for communicating God's Word, Bryan has become known as a trusted partner to ministries large and small. His passion and gift is moving ministries and people forward, toward God's best. Bryan is married to his best friend, Ashley; they live in Nashville, Tennessee.

CONTENTS

A MESSAGE TO READERS

From time to time, all of us must deal with difficult people—it's simply the price we pay for being actively engaged in life. So, unless you live alone, with absolutely no contact with the outside world, you will encounter people with prickly personalities, terrible temperaments, irritating habits, and infuriating character flaws. Whether you like it or not, these folks manage to weave themselves into the fabric of your life, and you must find ways to manage the ensuing headaches, heartbreaks, chaos, and stress. The ideas found in this text can help you survive these difficult relationships without sacrificing your sanity or compromising your Christian faith.

God has given you a book of instructions upon which you can and must depend. That book, of course, is the Holy Bible. The Bible is a priceless gift, a tool that God intends for you to use in every aspect of your life. Yet sometimes you may be tempted to treat the Bible less like a guidebook and more like a history book. Please don't make that mistake! Instead, trust God's promises and use His Word as an indispensable guide for life here on earth and for life eternal.

Sometime soon, perhaps this very day, you'll encounter someone who disrupts your life and unsettles your psyche. When you do, consider the ideas on the following pages to be God's instructions for handling that tough interpersonal relationship. Your heavenly Father is ready, willing, and able to help you manage the minor inconveniences and major stumbling blocks of everyday life. And, with His help, all things are possible—even the daunting task of dealing with difficult people.

SIX STEPS FOR DEALING WITH DIFFICULT PEOPLE

Recognize that as long as you live, you're going to encounter difficult people. So you might as well learn how to deal with them now.

Understand that emotions are contagious. If you let them, difficult people can stir up negative emotions that are harmful to your spiritual and emotional health. Don't let them.

Understand that you can learn to control your emotions and deal more effectively with difficult people. It may take training and practice, but if you sincerely want to gain better control over your emotions, you can do it. With God, all things are possible.

When you encounter difficult people, rely on God for strength and keep your emotional distance. The enemy wants you to behave like a non-Christian. God wants you to follow in the footsteps of His Son. Trust God.

Don't compromise yourself. Try to be understanding, and try to be kind, but don't give in to unreasonable requests, and don't let anyone convince you to compromise your ethics or forsake your conscience.

Forgive and forget as soon as possible. Difficult people come; difficult people go. Forgive them and move on as quickly as you can, so you can return to a more positive, peaceful emotional state.

1

THE QUESTION

It seems like I'm always bumping into
people who seem determined
to make my life difficult. Why do I seem to
encounter so many difficult people?

THE ANSWER

We can never be sure why God allows us
to encounter difficult people. But we can be
certain He has a plan for our lives that includes
the spiritual growth that inevitably occurs when
we learn how to deal with difficult people
and troubling situations.

———〰———

*And we know that God causes all things to work
together for good to those who love God, to those
who are called according to His purpose.*

Romans 8:28 NASB

WE ALL ENCOUNTER DIFFICULT PEOPLE

Teach me Your way, O Lord,
and lead me in a level path.
PSALM 27:11 NASB

Unless you lead a solitary life, living alone and never leaving your own home, you'll encounter difficult people. Lots of difficult people. Why? Because they're everywhere: in all walks of life, in all economic strata, in every profession, and in every large institution. Typically, you don't invite these folks to participate in your day or your life. They simply show up, sometimes out of nowhere, asking contentious questions, ignoring the positives, and focusing on the negatives, making you and everybody around you uncomfortable. Often difficult people arrive in a hurry and leave just as quickly. But sometimes these folks become permanent fixtures; sometimes they're people we can't escape.

So, what should we do about the difficult people who inhabit our lives and invade our psyches? First, we should realize that God sometimes uses difficult people to achieve His plans for our lives. These people have much to teach us about ourselves, so we should examine every encounter to determine whether God is using our adversaries to advance our own spiritual growth.

In addition to teaching us valuable lessons about life, difficult people also teach us about spiritual virtues such as patience, perseverance, forgiveness, and courage. Often, our antagonists teach us lessons we could learn in no other way.

The ideas in this text are intended to help you navigate difficult personal relationships without compromising your ethics or your faith. So, instead of fretting about the prickly personalities who inhabit your life, open your heart to God's guidance and His love. Listen to Him, and treat all of His children with love and respect. When you do, you'll be a blessing to all those whom God has seen fit to place along your path.

MORE FROM GOD'S WORD

And whenever you stand praying, if you have anything against anyone, forgive him, so that your Father in heaven will also forgive you your wrongdoing.
MARK 11:25 HCSB

Everyone must be quick to hear, slow to speak, and slow to anger, for man's anger does not accomplish God's righteousness.
JAMES 1:19–20 HCSB

He who says he is in the light, and hates his brother, is in darkness until now.
1 JOHN 2:9 NKJV

A patient spirit is better than a proud spirit.
ECCLESIASTES 7:8 HCSB

Trust in the LORD with all your heart, and lean not on your own understanding; in all your ways acknowledge Him, and He shall direct your paths.
PROVERBS 3:5–6 NKJV

MORE THOUGHTS

*Whatever a person may be like, we must
still love them because we love God.*

JOHN CALVIN

*We are all fallen creatures and
all very hard to live with.*

C. S. LEWIS

*If you are a Christian, you are not a citizen of this
world trying to get to heaven; you are a citizen of
heaven making your way through this world.*

VANCE HAVNER

*Give me such love for God and men as will
blot out all hatred and bitterness.*

DIETRICH BONHOEFFER

*How often should you forgive the other person?
Only as many times as you want
God to forgive you!*

MARIE T. FREEMAN

REMEMBER THIS

For the rest of your life, you'll encounter people with prickly personalities, so you might as well learn how to deal with them now. You can take comfort in the fact that, with God's help, you can learn how to deal with difficult personalities in ways that are pleasing to Him and helpful to you.

GET PRACTICAL

Think of several recent situations in which you've encountered people who had prickly personalities. How did you deal with them? How could you have handled things better?

—⧖—

A CONVERSATION STARTER

Talk to a friend about ways in which you've customarily dealt with difficult people, and talk about better strategies for dealing with them in the future.

YOUR THOUGHTS
DEALING WITH
DIFFICULT PEOPLE

Write down the ways that you typically respond to people with difficult personalities. What are the positive aspects of your typical response? What are the negative aspects?

....

....

....

....

....

....

....

....

....

2

THE QUESTION

It seems like I'm always dealing with people who have difficult personalities. Why does God allow this to happen?

THE ANSWER

God has His own reasons for allowing events to unfold as they do. Sometimes He allows us to endure difficult circumstances in order for us to acquire lessons that we could learn in no other way.

For my thoughts are not your thoughts, neither are your ways my ways, declares the LORD.... You will go out in joy and be led forth in peace; the mountains and hills will burst into song before you, and all the trees of the field will clap their hands.

ISAIAH 55:8, 12 NIV

GOD IS IN CONTROL

He is the LORD. He will do
what He thinks is good.
1 SAMUEL 3:18 HCSB

Why does God allow difficult people to cross our paths and, potentially, ruffle our emotions? He does it for specific reasons that are known only to Him, but of this we can be sure: He always has our best interests at heart.

God created our universe, and He rules it according to plans that are His and His alone. Through His Word, He makes promises that He will most certainly keep throughout eternity. But sometimes God's plans are simply impossible for us to understand. Why are some people burdened with difficult personalities? We can't be sure. And why do bad things happen to good people? We don't know. But God does. And we must trust His perfect plan, even when we cannot understand it.

Your heavenly Father is sovereign. He reigns over His creation, and He reigns over your little corner of that creation, too. Your challenge is to recognize God's sovereignty and to trust His promises. Often, the Lord will not always reveal Himself as quickly—or as clearly—as you would like. But rest assured: God is in control, and He desires to lead you along a path of His choosing. Your challenge is to trust, to listen, to learn, and to follow.

So, the next time you encounter a person with a prickly personality, don't fret and don't complain. Instead, stay calm and ask God for His guidance. When you do, you can be sure that the emotional storm will pass, probably sooner than you think.

MORE FROM GOD'S WORD

The earth is the LORD's, and everything in it.
The world and all its people belong to him.
PSALM 24:1 NLT

The LORD is good to those who depend on him,
to those who search for him. So it is good to
wait quietly for salvation from the LORD.
LAMENTATIONS 3:25–26 NLT

Should we accept only good from God
and not adversity?
JOB 2:10 HCSB

For now we see in a mirror, dimly, but then
face to face. Now I know in part, but then
I shall know just as I also am known.
1 CORINTHIANS 13:12 NKJV

Obey God and be at peace with him;
this is the way to happiness.
JOB 22:21 NCV

MORE THOUGHTS

God is in control, and therefore in everything I can give thanks—not because of the situation but because of the One who directs and rules over it.

KAY ARTHUR

One of the marks of spiritual maturity is the quiet confidence that God is in control, without the need to understand why He does what He does.

CHARLES SWINDOLL

If not a sparrow falls upon the ground without your Father, you have reason to see that the smallest events of your career are arranged by Him.

C. H. SPURGEON

The presence of hope in the invincible sovereignty of God drives out fear.

JOHN PIPER

What an incredible witness it is to a lost and fearful society when the Christian acts like a child of God, living under the loving sovereignty of the heavenly Father.

HENRY BLACKABY

REMEMBER THIS

God is in control of His world and your world. Trust Him. If you're dealing with a difficult person or adverse circumstances, remember that the Lord is always by your side. Rely upon Him. Learn from Him.

GET PRACTICAL

The next time you encounter a difficult person, remind yourself that God is in control and that He has a good reason—His reason—for bringing this person into your life.

—๛—

A CONVERSATION STARTER

Talk to a friend about the lessons you both can learn when you accept God's sovereignty and trust His plans.

YOUR THOUGHTS
GOD IS IN CONTROL

Write down your thoughts about God's infinite wisdom, His infinite power, and His influence on the events of your everyday life.

....

....

....

....

....

....

....

....

....

....

3

THE QUESTION

When I'm around people with troubling personalities, my emotions seem to go haywire. Why does this always seem to happen to me?

THE ANSWER

Emotions are contagious. When we're around people who are emotionally distraught, we're tempted to become upset, too, unless we maintain a safe psychological distance from the emotional outburst.

*These things I have spoken to you,
that in Me you may have peace. In the world
you will have tribulation; but be of good cheer,
I have overcome the world.*
JOHN 16:33 NKJV

EMOTIONS ARE CONTAGIOUS

People with quick tempers cause trouble, but those who control their tempers stop a quarrel.

PROVERBS 15:18 NCV

Time and again, the Bible instructs us to live by faith. Yet, despite our best intentions, negative feelings can rob us of the peace and abundance that could be ours—and should be ours— through Christ. When anger, frustration, impatience, or anxiety separates us from the spiritual blessings that God has in store, we must rethink our priorities. And we must place our faith above our feelings.

Negative emotions, like their positive counterparts, are contagious. So, it's not surprising that when you encounter people with difficult personalities, you may experience the same emotions they're feeling. If the other person is angry, you may become angry, too. If the other person is pessimistic, you may soon feel the same way. If the other person is highly emotional, you may have trouble controlling your own emotions.

Human emotions are highly variable, decidedly unpredictable, and often unreliable. Our emotions change like the weather, but they're less predictable and far more fickle! So we must learn to live by faith, not by the ups and downs of our own emotional roller coasters.

Who's pulling your emotional strings? Are you allowing highly emotional people or highly charged situations to dictate your moods, or are you wiser than that?

Sometime during the coming day, you may encounter a tough situation or a difficult person. And as a result, you may be gripped by a strong negative emotion. Distrust it. Rein it in. Test it. And turn it over to the Lord. Your emotions will inevitably change; God will not. So, trust Him completely. When you do, you'll be surprised at how quickly those negative feelings can evaporate into thin air.

MORE FROM GOD'S WORD

All bitterness, anger and wrath, shouting and slander must be removed from you, along with all malice. And be kind and compassionate to one another, forgiving one another, just as God also forgave you in Christ.
EPHESIANS 4:31–32 HCSB

And let the peace of God rule in your hearts, to which also you were called in one body; and be thankful.
COLOSSIANS 3:15 NKJV

For this very reason, make every effort to supplement your faith with goodness, goodness with knowledge, knowledge with self-control, self-control with endurance, endurance with godliness.
2 PETER 1:5–6 HCSB

Enthusiasm without knowledge is not good. If you act too quickly, you might make a mistake.
PROVERBS 19:2 NCV

Grow a wise heart—you'll do yourself a favor; keep a clear head—you'll find a good life.
PROVERBS 19:8 MSG

MORE THOUGHTS

Our emotions can lie to us, and we need to counter our emotions with truth.

BILLY GRAHAM

Our feelings do not affect God's facts.

AMY CARMICHAEL

A life lived in God is not lived on the plane of feelings, but of the will.

ELISABETH ELLIOT

Feelings are like chemicals; the more you analyze them, the worse they smell.

CHARLES KINGSLEY

It is Christ who is to be exalted, not our feelings. We will know Him by obedience, not by emotions. Our love will be shown by obedience, not by how good we feel about God at a given moment.

ELISABETH ELLIOT

REMEMBER THIS

Human emotions are highly contagious, so when you're around people with difficult personalities, you're more likely to become upset. But if you're mentally prepared, you can resist negative emotions by making a conscious effort to stay calm.

GET PRACTICAL

The next time you encounter a difficult person, be aware of your emotions. If you begin to get upset, worried, frustrated, or angry, catch yourself, take a deep breath, and calm yourself down. Don't allow the other person's emotions to become your emotions.

A CONVERSATION STARTER

Talk to a friend about ways you both can stay calm when the people around you are upset or angry or both.

YOUR THOUGHTS
ABOUT EMOTIONS

Write down your thoughts about the power and the impact of positive and negative emotions.

....

....

....

....

....

....

....

....

....

4

THE QUESTION

I don't want to be spiritually stuck. I want to
keep growing and maturing as a Christian.
How can I do this?

THE ANSWER

Spiritual maturity is a journey, not a destination.
You can, and should, continue to mature in your
faith through every stage of life. To do so, you
must ask for God's help and follow His instructions.
When you do your part, He'll certainly do His part.

*Run away from infantile indulgence.
Run after mature righteousness—faith, love,
peace—joining those who are in honest
and serious prayer before God.*

2 TIMOTHY 2:22 MSG

DIFFICULT PEOPLE HELP US GROW

So let us stop going over the basic teachings about Christ again and again. Let us go on instead and become mature in our understanding.

HEBREWS 6:1 NLT

People with difficult personalities can help us learn valuable lessons, lessons we might not learn from other easygoing folks. Difficult people teach us about patience; they teach us about forgiveness; they teach us how to be strong, and how to stand up for ourselves. Our encounters with difficult people can help us grow; they can help us mature; and they can give us valuable insights into the human condition.

As a Christian, you should never stop growing. No matter your age, no matter your circumstances, you have opportunities to learn and opportunities to serve. Wherever you happen to be, God is there, too, and He wants to bless you with an expanding array of spiritual gifts. Your job is to let Him.

The path to spiritual maturity unfolds day by day, during good times and in frustrating times. Through prayer, through Bible study, and through obedience to God's Word, you can strengthen your relationship with Him. The more you focus on the Father, the more blessings you'll receive. So, the next time you encounter a person with a prickly personality, consider it an adventure in spiritual growth. And consider the possibility that God may be trying to teach you a very important lesson, a lesson He knows you need to learn.

MORE FROM GOD'S WORD

*I remind you to fan into flames the
spiritual gift God gave you.*
2 Timothy 1:6 NLT

*And be not conformed to this world:
but be ye transformed by the renewing of
your mind, that ye may prove what is that good,
and acceptable, and perfect, will of God.*
Romans 12:2 KJV

*Leave inexperience behind, and you will live;
pursue the way of understanding.*
Proverbs 9:6 HCSB

*But endurance must do its complete work,
so that you may be mature and complete,
lacking nothing.*
James 1:4 HCSB

*But grow in the grace and knowledge of our
Lord and Savior Jesus Christ. To Him be the glory
both now and forever. Amen.*
2 Peter 3:18 NKJV

MORE THOUGHTS

God's ultimate goal for your life on earth is not comfort, but character development. He wants you to grow up spiritually and become like Christ.

RICK WARREN

Grow, dear friends, but grow, I beseech you, in God's way, which is the only true way.

HANNAH WHITALL SMITH

Mark it down. You will never go where God is not.

MAX LUCADO

The vigor of our spiritual life will be in exact proportion to the place held by the Bible in our life and thoughts.

GEORGE MÜLLER

God will help us become the people we are meant to be, if only we will ask Him.

HANNAH WHITALL SMITH

REMEMBER THIS

You can learn something from everyone, which includes people with prickly personalities. Sometimes difficult people can teach you valuable lessons about yourself and your world.

GET PRACTICAL

The next time you encounter a person with a difficult personality, ask yourself, What is God trying to teach me right now?

A CONVERSATION STARTER

Talk to a friend about the life lessons you both have learned from people with difficult personalities.

YOUR THOUGHTS
SPIRITUAL GROWTH AND MATURITY

Write down some ways in which difficult people can help you grow both spiritually and emotionally.

....

....

....

....

....

....

....

....

....

....

5

THE QUESTION

It seems like I've still got so much to learn about dealing with difficult people. Will I ever be able to figure it out?

THE ANSWER

Of course you can always learn better strategies for dealing with difficult people. And while you're at it, you'll probably gain insights that will help you navigate other relationships, too.

In God's economy, whether He is making a flower or a human soul, nothing ever comes to nothing. The losses are His way of accomplishing the gains.

ELISABETH ELLIOT

DIFFICULT PEOPLE TEACH US ABOUT OURSELVES

Wisdom is the principal thing; therefore get wisdom.
And in all your getting, get understanding.
PROVERBS 4:7 NKJV

Difficult people can teach us invaluable lessons about ourselves. Those troublesome people, with their prickly personalities, can expose our own personality quirks and vulnerabilities. If we pay careful attention to the way we respond to various personality styles, we can learn better ways to respond and better strategies for managing troublesome relationships.

When it comes to learning life's lessons, we can do things either the easy way or the hard way. The easy way can be summed up as follows: When life teaches us a lesson, we learn it...the first time! Unfortunately, too many of us learn much more slowly than that.

God wants us to grow spiritually, emotionally, and intellectually. But He doesn't force us to learn. When we resist His instruction, the Lord continues to teach us, whether we like it or not. Our challenge, then, is to discern God's lessons from the experiences of everyday life. Hopefully we will learn His lessons sooner rather than later, because the sooner we do, the sooner He can move on to the next lesson, and the next, and the next....

MORE FROM GOD'S WORD

Anyone who listens to my teaching and follows it is wise, like a person who builds a house on solid rock.
MATTHEW 7:24 NLT

Joyful is the person who finds wisdom, the one who gains understanding.
PROVERBS 3:13 NLT

Teach me Your way, Yahweh, and I will live by Your truth. Give me an undivided mind to fear Your name.
PSALM 86:11 HCSB

Enthusiasm without knowledge is not good. If you act too quickly, you might make a mistake.
PROVERBS 19:2 NCV

Commit yourself to instruction; listen carefully to words of knowledge.
PROVERBS 23:12 NLT

MORE THOUGHTS

A time of trouble and darkness is meant to teach you lessons you desperately need.

LETTIE COWMAN

Every day we live is a priceless gift of God, loaded with possibilities to learn something new, to gain fresh insights.

DALE EVANS ROGERS

Life is not a holiday, but an education. And the one eternal lesson for all of us is how we can love.

HENRY DRUMMOND

Learning makes a man fit company for himself.

THOMAS FULLER

True learning can take place at every age of life, and it doesn't have to be in the curriculum plan.

SUZANNE DALE EZELL

REMEMBER THIS

You still have lots to learn about yourself. Sometimes God allows us to endure difficult circumstances so that we might grow and mature as Christians.

GET PRACTICAL

Think of an important lesson you've learned from a person with a difficult personality. How did that lesson help you become a better person and a better Christian?

A CONVERSATION STARTER

Talk to a friend about ways in which you both have matured during the last few years. Have difficult people ever taught you lessons you couldn't have learned from other easygoing folks?

YOUR THOUGHTS
LIFETIME LEARNING

Write down your thoughts about the joys and the rewards of lifetime learning.

....

....

....

....

....

....

....

....

....

....

....

6

THE QUESTION

I know I should be kind to all people,
not just the ones who are easy to get along with.
But sometimes it's hard to overlook the obvious
personality flaws of people who stretch
my patience to the limit. What does the Bible
instruct me to do?

THE ANSWER

The Bible teaches us to treat all people as we
would wish to be treated if we were in their shoes.
It's hard, but not impossible, to treat everyone
with respect, even the people who infuriate us.

Honor all people. Love the brotherhood.
Fear God. Honor the king.

1 Peter 2:17 NKJV

ASSUME THE BEST
AND BE KIND

*Therefore, whatever you want men
to do to you, do also to them, for this is
the Law and the Prophets.*
MATTHEW 7:12 NKJV

In Matthew 7:12, Jesus instructed us to treat others as we wish
to be treated. But sometimes this is hard. When we encounter difficult people with troublesome personalities, we may be
tempted to respond in ways that are decidedly unkind. We may
respond emotionally, or negatively, or angrily. But God's Word
teaches us to be patient and compassionate, not impatient and
hostile. As Christians, we are held to a higher standard: we must
attempt to reflect Christ's love to all the people we meet, not just
the ones with pleasing personalities.

Kindness is a choice. Sometimes, when we feel happy or
prosperous, we find it easy to be kind. Other times, when we
are tired or discouraged, we can scarcely summon the energy to
utter a single kind word. But God clearly intends that we make
the conscious choice to treat others with kindness and respect,
no matter our circumstances, no matter our emotions.

The next time you encounter someone with a prickly personality, be compassionate, be forgiving, assume the best, and
treat that person as you'd wish to be treated. When you weave
the thread of kindness into the very fabric of your day, you'll
give a priceless gift to others and you'll give glory to the One
who gave His life for you. As a believer, you must do no less.

MORE FROM GOD'S WORD

*Be kind to one another, tender-hearted,
forgiving each other, just as God in Christ
also has forgiven you.*
EPHESIANS 4:32 NASB

*And let us not grow weary while doing good, for in
due season we shall reap if we do not lose heart.*
GALATIANS 6:9 NKJV

*A new commandment I give unto you,
that ye love one another; as I have loved you,
that ye also love one another.*
JOHN 13:34 KJV

*Who is wise and has understanding among you?
He should show his works by good conduct
with wisdom's gentleness.*
JAMES 3:13 HCSB

*Assuredly, I say to you, inasmuch as you
did it to one of the least of these My brethren,
you did it to Me.*
MATTHEW 25:40 NKJV

MORE THOUGHTS

If my heart is right with God,
every human being is my neighbor.
OSWALD CHAMBERS

Love, joy, peace, patience, kindness, goodness,
faithfulness, gentleness, and self-control.
To these I commit my day.
MAX LUCADO

When we bring sunshine into the lives of others,
we're warmed by it ourselves. When we spill
a little happiness, it splashes on us.
BARBARA JOHNSON

One of the greatest things a man can do
for his heavenly Father is to be kind to
some of His other children.
HENRY DRUMMOND

Do all the good you can by all the means you can
in all the places you can at all the times you can to
all the people you can as long as ever you can.
JOHN WESLEY

REMEMBER THIS

When assessing the motives of other people, only God is the final Judge. Your duty, as a Christian, is to love your neighbor, even if he has a difficult personality.

GET PRACTICAL

Think of a time when you were too quick to judge the motives of another person. How did you feel then? How will you react in the future?

—⁓—

A CONVERSATION STARTER

Talk to a friend about the need to look for the best in others, even when it's a challenge.

YOUR THOUGHTS
ABOUT THE GOLDEN RULE

Write down your thoughts about practical ways you can apply the Golden Rule when you're dealing with difficult people.

....

....

....

....

....

....

....

....

....

....

....

7

THE QUESTION

Sometimes I feel like my strength is almost gone. What can I do about that?

THE ANSWER

When you need strength, the first place you should turn is to God. So, pray often; ask for His guidance; and ask Him to help you establish your priorities. Don't try to do everything or please everyone. Simply do your best and leave the rest up to Him.

We can be tired, weary, and emotionally distraught, but after spending time alone with God, we find that He injects into our bodies energy, power, and strength.
CHARLES STANLEY

WHERE TO FIND STRENGTH

He gives strength to the weary, and to him
who lacks might He increases power.
Isaiah 40:29 NASB

Dealing with a difficult person can be a draining experience. So, where should you go to recharge your emotional batteries? The medicine cabinet? The health food store? The gym? These places may offer a temporary energy boost, but the best place to turn for strength and solace isn't down the hall or at the mall; it's as near as your next breath. The best Source of strength is God.

God's love for you never changes, and neither does His support. From the cradle to the grave, He has promised to give you the strength you need to meet the challenges of life. He has promised to guide you and protect you if you let Him. But He also expects you to do your part.

Today provides yet another opportunity to partake in the strength that only God can provide. You do so by tuning your heart to Him through prayer, obedience, and trust. People can be difficult, and life can be challenging, but fear not. Whatever your challenge, God can give you the strength to face it and overcome it. Let Him.

MORE FROM GOD'S WORD

Have faith in the Lord your God, and you
will stand strong. Have faith in his prophets,
and you will succeed.
2 Chronicles 20:20 NCV

Be strong and courageous, and do the work.
Don't be afraid or discouraged,
for the Lord God, my God, is with you.
He won't leave you or forsake you.
1 Chronicles 28:20 HCSB

The Lord is my strength and my song;
He has become my salvation.
Exodus 15:2 HCSB

My grace is sufficient for you, for my power
is made perfect in weakness.
2 Corinthians 12:9 NIV

I can do all things through Christ
who strengthens me.
Philippians 4:13 NKJV

MORE THOUGHTS

The strength that we claim from God's Word does not depend on circumstances. Circumstances will be difficult, but our strength will be sufficient.

CORRIE TEN BOOM

Faith is a strong power, mastering any difficulty in the strength of the Lord who made heaven and earth.

CORRIE TEN BOOM

The truth is, God's strength is fully revealed when our strength is depleted.

LIZ CURTIS HIGGS

God will give us the strength and resources we need to live through any situation in life that He ordains.

BILLY GRAHAM

God is in control. He may not take away trials or make detours for us, but He strengthens us through them.

BILLY GRAHAM

REMEMBER THIS

Your heavenly Father can give you all the strength you need to handle any situation He ordains. He will never give you a greater burden than you can bear.

GET PRACTICAL

If your emotional batteries are depleted, slow down, get more rest, and—most importantly—turn your troubles over to God. When you turn everything over to Him, you'll feel stronger.

A CONVERSATION STARTER

Talk to a friend about times when you've both gained strength from your faith.

YOUR THOUGHTS
FINDING STRENGTH

Write down your thoughts about the best ways to find the strength you need to deal more effectively with difficult people.

....

....

....

....

....

....

....

....

....

....

8

THE QUESTION

Sometimes difficult people attack my sense of self-worth. What does the Bible say about that?

THE ANSWER

Time and again, God's Word warns against the danger of pride. So, look within yourself to be sure that your own sense of pride isn't interfering with God's plan for your life.

A man wrapped up in himself makes a very small package.

BEN FRANKLIN

BEWARE OF PRIDE

A patient spirit is better than a proud spirit.
ECCLESIASTES 7:8 HCSB

People with difficult personalities often incite us by threatening one of our most prized possessions: our pride. They belittle us in some way, and we're tempted to react instinctively by striking back in anger. That's one reason, but not the only reason, that pride is such a dangerous emotion.

If we read God's Word and trust it, we will clearly understand the perils of pride. Time and again He warns us that pride, indeed, comes before a fall. But sometimes our feelings of pride are so subtle that we fail to recognize them for what they are, mistaking unhealthy pride for "self-confidence," or "self-assurance," or "self-respect."

Self-confidence and self-assurance are wonderful traits, as long as we keep them in check. But if we allow our feelings of self-importance to cause us to disobey any of God's commandments, we invite His displeasure.

So, the next time you encounter a difficult person who attacks your sense of self-worth, stand up for yourself without resorting to angry outbursts or name calling. Just because another person behaves badly doesn't mean that you should, too.

MORE FROM GOD'S WORD

God resists the proud,
but gives grace to the humble.
JAMES 4:6 HCSB

You save the humble, but you bring down
those who are proud.
2 SAMUEL 22:28 NCV

For whoever exalts himself will be humbled,
and whoever humbles himself will be exalted.
MATTHEW 23:12 NIV

When pride comes, disgrace follows,
but with humility comes wisdom.
PROVERBS 11:2 HCSB

Do nothing out of rivalry or conceit, but in humility
consider others as more important than yourselves.
PHILIPPIANS 2:3 HCSB

MORE THOUGHTS

If you wish to be miserable, think much about yourself; about what you want, what you like, what respect people ought to pay you, and what people think of you.

CHARLES KINGSLEY

Pride builds walls between people; humility builds bridges.

RICK WARREN

It is very easy to overestimate the importance of our own achievements in comparison with what we owe others.

DIETRICH BONHOEFFER

All pride is idolatry.

JOHN WESLEY

Pride gets no pleasure out of having something, only out of having more of it than the next man.

C. S. LEWIS

REMEMBER THIS

Everything you have—all of your talents, abilities, and possessions—come from God. Give Him thanks, and give Him the glory.

GET PRACTICAL

Think about times when your actions were motivated by pride. Now think of better ways to react in the future.

A CONVERSATION STARTER

Talk to a friend about the dangers of pride: how it can hurt you and how it can hurt others.

YOUR THOUGHTS
ABOUT PRIDE

Write down your thoughts about the dangers and draw-backs of pride.

9

THE QUESTION

Sometimes it's easy for me to be the one who gets angry. What does the Bible say about anger?

THE ANSWER

The Bible warns us time and again that the word anger is only one letter different from the word danger. So, the next time you're confronted by a difficult person and you're tempted to lose your cool, walk away before you get carried away.

*We must meet our disappointments,
our malicious enemies, our provoking friends,
our trials of every sort, with an attitude of surrender
and trust. We must rise above them in Christ
so they lose their power to harm us.*

HANNAH WHITALL SMITH

ANGER MEANS DANGER

Everyone must be quick to hear, slow to speak, and slow to anger, for man's anger does not accomplish God's righteousness.

JAMES 1:19–20 HCSB

People with difficult personalities can hurt our feelings, sabotage our plans, and disrupt our lives. When we've been hurt badly, we don't forget easily. When we can identify the person who hurt us, we naturally focus our ire on the perpetrator. Unless we can find the inner strength to forgive that person, we're likely to internalize our anger for years, for decades, or even for a lifetime. Anger turned inward is always detrimental to our spiritual health and disruptive to our lives. And that's one reason—but not the only reason—that we should learn how to forgive other people quickly and completely. To do otherwise will result in needless anger and inner turmoil.

First Peter 5:8–9 warns, "Stay alert! Watch out for your great enemy, the devil. He prowls around like a roaring lion, looking for someone to devour. Stand firm against him, and be strong in your faith" (NLT). And of this you can be sure: Your adversary will use an unforgiving heart, and the inevitable anger that dwells within it, to sabotage your life and undermine your faith. To be safe, you must cleanse your heart, and you must forgive. You must say yes to God, yes to mercy, yes to love, and no to anger.

MORE FROM GOD'S WORD

A hot-tempered man stirs up conflict,
but a man slow to anger calms strife.
PROVERBS 15:18 HCSB

But now you must also put away all the following:
anger, wrath, malice, slander, and filthy language
from your mouth.
COLOSSIANS 3:8 HCSB

But I tell you that anyone who is angry with his
brother will be subject to judgment.
MATTHEW 5:22 NIV

He who is slow to wrath has great understanding,
but he who is impulsive exalts folly.
PROVERBS 14:29 NKJV

Do not let the sun go down on your anger,
and do not give the devil an opportunity.
EPHESIANS 4:26–27 NASB

MORE THOUGHTS

Hence it is not enough to deal with the Temper.
We must go to the source, and change
the inmost nature, and the angry humors
will die away of themselves.

HENRY DRUMMOND

Hot heads and cold hearts
never solved anything.

BILLY GRAHAM

Frustration is not the will of God. There is time to do
anything and everything that God wants us to do.

ELISABETH ELLIOT

Anger and bitterness—whatever the cause—
only end up hurting us.
Turn that anger over to Christ.

BILLY GRAHAM

Life is too short to spend it being angry,
bored, or dull.

BARBARA JOHNSON

REMEMBER THIS

Emotions are highly contagious, and angry encounters almost never have happy endings. So, if someone is ranting, raving, or worse, you should exercise your right to leave the scene of the argument.

GET PRACTICAL

If you think you're about to explode in anger, slow down, take a deep breath, and walk away from the scene of the argument. It's better to walk away—and keep walking—than it is to blurt out angry words that can't be taken back.

—⚍—

A CONVERSATION STARTER

Talk to a friend about the consequences of angry outbursts. How do they impact others? How do they impact your own emotional health?

YOUR THOUGHTS
ABOUT ANGER

Write down your thoughts about the inevitable problems that result from anger that's either expressed in inappropriate ways or held inside.

_____

_____

_____

_____

_____

_____

_____

_____

_____

_____

10

THE QUESTION

When I encounter difficult people, I often experience negative emotions such as anger, resentment, and even hatred. What should I do?

THE ANSWER

God wants you to guard your heart from any distractions or temptations that might cause you to stray from His path. When you encounter tough times or difficult people, turn your thoughts and prayers toward your Creator.

It is the thoughts and intents of the heart that shape a person's life.

JOHN ELDREDGE

GUARD YOUR HEART

*Guard your heart above all else,
for it is the source of life.*
PROVERBS 4:23 HCSB

Difficult people tempt us to respond in vindictive, aggressive ways. Yet God's Word is clear: we are to guard our hearts "above all else." So, how should we respond to the prickly personalities that complicate our lives and rouse our emotions? We must do so fairly, honestly, and maturely, and we must never betray our Christian beliefs.

Here in the twenty-first century, distractions, frustrations, and angry eruptions are woven into the fabric of everyday life. Many famous people seem to take pride in discourteous behavior, and social media has dramatically increased our contact with troubled personalities. As believers, we must remain vigilant. Not only must we resist Satan when he confronts us, but we must also avoid the people and the places where Satan can most easily tempt us.

Do you seek God's peace and His blessings? Then guard your heart above all else. When you encounter a difficult person and you're tempted to lash out in anger, hold your tongue. When you're faced with a difficult choice or a powerful temptation, seek God's counsel and trust the counsel He gives. When you're uncertain of your next step, take a deep breath, calm yourself, and follow in the footsteps of God's only begotten Son. Invite God into your heart and live according to His commandments. When you do, you will be blessed today, and tomorrow, and forever.

MORE FROM GOD'S WORD

The pure in heart are blessed,
because they will see God.
MATTHEW 5:8 HCSB

Flee from youthful passions, and pursue
righteousness, faith, love, and peace, along with
those who call on the Lord from a pure heart.
2 TIMOTHY 2:22 HCSB

The peace of God, which surpasses all
understanding, will guard your hearts and minds
through Christ Jesus.
PHILIPPIANS 4:7 NKJV

Those who obey his commands live in him, and he
in them. And this is how we know that he lives in us:
We know it by the Spirit he gave us.
1 JOHN 3:24 NIV

Finally, brothers, whatever is true, whatever is
noble, whatever is right, whatever is pure, whatever
is lovely, whatever is admirable—if anything is
excellent or praiseworthy—think about such things.
PHILIPPIANS 4:8 NIV

MORE THOUGHTS

*No matter how many pleasures Satan offers you,
his ultimate intention is to ruin you. Your destruction
is his highest priority.*

ERWIN LUTZER

*Our fight is not against any physical enemy;
it is against organizations and powers that are
spiritual. We must struggle against sin all our lives,
but we are assured we will win.*

CORRIE TEN BOOM

*Our battles are first won or lost in the
secret places of our will in God's presence,
never in full view of the world.*

OSWALD CHAMBERS

*There is no neutral ground in the universe:
Every square inch, every split second, is claimed
by God and counterclaimed by Satan.*

C. S. LEWIS

*The insight that relates to God comes from purity
of heart, not from clearness of intellect.*

OSWALD CHAMBERS

REMEMBER THIS

God wants you to think carefully about the things you do and the people with whom you associate. When you do these things, you'll guard your heart, and you'll be blessed.

GET PRACTICAL

Make note of any time-gobbling distractions or spirit-deflating temptations that threaten your spiritual health. Then ask God to help you guard your heart against them.

A CONVERSATION STARTER

Talk to a friend about the blessings that God bestows upon His obedient servants.

YOUR THOUGHTS
GUARD YOUR HEART

Write down some things you can do to guard your heart when confronting difficult people.

....

....

....

....

....

....

....

....

....

....

....

....

....

....

11

THE QUESTION

When I'm overcome by anxiety and worries,
what should I do? And where should I turn?

THE ANSWER

Carefully divide your areas of concern into two
categories: those things you can control and
those you cannot control. Once you've done this,
spend your time working to resolve the things you
can control, and entrust everything else to God.

Claim all of God's promises in the Bible.
Your sins, your worries, your life—
you may cast them all on Him.

CORRIE TEN BOOM

BEYOND WORRY

Therefore do not worry about tomorrow,
for tomorrow will worry about its own things.
Sufficient for the day is its own trouble.
MATTHEW 6:34 NKJV

Because you have the ability to think, you also have the ability to worry. Even if you're a very faithful Christian, you may be plagued by occasional periods of discouragement and doubt, especially if you're caught in an intense relationship with a difficult person. Even though you trust God's promise of salvation—even though you sincerely believe in God's love and protection—you may find yourself upset by the continual frustrations generated by people with prickly personalities.

Where is the best place to take your worries? Take them to God. Take your troubles to Him; take your fears to Him; take your doubts to Him; take your weaknesses to Him; take your frustrations to Him, and leave them all there. Seek protection from the One who offers you eternal salvation; build your spiritual house upon the Rock that cannot be moved. Then, perhaps, you will worry less and trust God more, and that's as it should be, because God is trustworthy and you are protected.

MORE FROM GOD'S WORD

*Peace I leave with you; My peace I give to you;
not as the world gives do I give to you. Do not let
your heart be troubled, nor let it be fearful.*
JOHN 14:27 NASB

*Do not be anxious about anything, but in
everything, by prayer and petition, with
thanksgiving, present your requests to God.*
PHILIPPIANS 4:6 NIV

*Let not your heart be troubled;
you believe in God, believe also in Me.*
JOHN 14:1 NKJV

*Cast all your anxiety on him
because he cares for you.*
1 PETER 5:7 NIV

*Cast your burden on the LORD,
and He shall sustain you; He shall never
permit the righteous to be moved.*
PSALM 55:22 NKJV

MORE THOUGHTS

Anxiety is not only a pain which we must ask God to assuage but also a weakness we must ask Him to pardon, for He's told us to take no care for the morrow.

C. S. LEWIS

Worry is the senseless process of cluttering up tomorrow's opportunities with leftover problems from today.

BARBARA JOHNSON

Tomorrow is busy worrying about itself; don't get tangled up in its worry-webs.

SARAH YOUNG

Pray, and let God worry.

MARTIN LUTHER

Do not worry about tomorrow. This is not a suggestion, but a command.

SARAH YOUNG

REMEMBER THIS

You have worries, but God has solutions. Your challenge is to trust Him to solve the problems that are simply too big for you to resolve on your own.

GET PRACTICAL

Divide your areas of concern into two categories: those you can control and those you can't. Focus on the former and refuse to waste time or energy worrying about the latter.

A CONVERSATION STARTER

Talk to a friend about ways in which you can trust God more and worry less.

YOUR THOUGHTS
ABOUT ANXIETY AND WORRY

Write down a few practical things you can do to overcome anxiety and worry.

....

....

....

....

....

....

....

....

....

....

....

12

THE QUESTION

It's hard not to be judgmental of other people, and it's hard not to judge their motives. What does the Bible say about judging others?

THE ANSWER

Your ability to judge others requires a divine insight that you simply do not have. So, do everybody (including yourself) a favor: don't judge.

Speak and act as those who will be judged by the law of freedom. For judgment is without mercy to the one who hasn't shown mercy. Mercy triumphs over judgment.

JAMES 2:12–13 HCSB

LET GOD BE THE JUDGE

Judge not, and you shall not be judged.
Condemn not, and you shall not be condemned.
Forgive, and you will be forgiven.

LUKE 6:37 NKJV

It's not surprising that we feel compelled to judge people with difficult personalities. The need to judge others seems woven into the very fabric of human consciousness. We mortals feel compelled to serve as informal judges and juries, pronouncing our own verdicts on the actions and perceived motivations of others, all the while excusing—or oftentimes hiding—our own shortcomings. But God's Word instructs us to let Him be the judge. He knows that we, with our limited knowledge and personal biases, are simply ill-equipped to assess the actions of others. The act of judging, then, becomes not only an act of futility, but also an affront to our Creator.

When Jesus came upon a woman who had been condemned by the Pharisees, He spoke not only to the people who had gathered there, but also to all future generations. Christ warned, "He that is without sin among you, let him first cast a stone at her" (John 8:7 KJV). The message is clear: because we are all sinners, we must refrain from the temptation to judge others.

So, the next time you're tempted to cast judgment on another human being, resist that temptation. God hasn't called you to be a judge; He's called you to be a witness.

MORE FROM GOD'S WORD

*Don't criticize one another, brothers. He who
criticizes a brother or judges his brother criticizes the
law and judges the law. But if you judge the law,
you are not a doer of the law but a judge.*
JAMES 4:11 HCSB

*Therefore, any one of you who judges is
without excuse. For when you judge another,
you condemn yourself, since you, the judge,
do the same things.*
ROMANS 2:1 HCSB

*Do everything without grumbling and arguing,
so that you may be blameless and pure.*
PHILIPPIANS 2:14–15 HCSB

*He who guards his lips guards his life,
but he who speaks rashly will come to ruin.*
PROVERBS 13:3 NIV

*Let the words of my mouth and the meditation
of my heart be acceptable in Your sight, O Lord,
my strength and my Redeemer.*
PSALM 19:14 NKJV

MORE THOUGHTS

Judging draws the judgment of others.

CATHERINE MARSHALL

*We must learn to regard people less
in the light of what they do or omit to do,
and more in light of what they suffer.*

DIETRICH BONHOEFFER

*Don't judge other people more harshly than you
want God to judge you.*

MARIE T. FREEMAN

*Yes, let God be the Judge. Your job today
is to be a witness.*

WARREN WIERSBE

*Oh, how horrible our sins look when they are
committed by someone else.*

CHARLES SWINDOLL

REMEMBER THIS

To judge others is a futile waste of energy and a clear disregard of God's teachings. To the extent that you judge others, so, too, will you be judged. So you must, to the best of your ability, refrain from judgmental thoughts and words.

GET PRACTICAL

If you catch yourself becoming overly judgmental, slow down long enough to interrupt those critical thoughts before they hijack your emotions and ruin your day.

—⚇—

A CONVERSATION STARTER

God instructs us to leave the judging up to Him. Talk to a friend about ways to resist the temptation of judging other people.

YOUR THOUGHTS
ABOUT JUDGING OTHER PEOPLE

Write down your thoughts about the dangers and pitfalls of judging other people.

....

....

....

....

....

....

....

....

....

....

13

THE QUESTION

Sometimes it's hard to be patient,
especially when people are difficult.
What advice can I find in God's Word?

THE ANSWER

The Bible teaches us that patience is better than
strength. When we're tempted to strike back at
the people who frustrate us, we should remember
that patience pays and impatience doesn't.

*Bear with the faults of others as
you would have them bear with yours.*

PHILLIPS BROOKS

BE PATIENT

A man's wisdom gives him patience;
it is to his glory to overlook an offense.
PROVERBS 19:11 NIV

God's Word teaches us to be patient and kind. We are commanded to love our neighbors, even when our neighbors aren't very neighborly. But being mere mortals, we fall short. We become easily frustrated with the shortcomings of others even though we are remarkably tolerant of our own failings.

We live in an imperfect world inhabited by imperfect friends, imperfect acquaintances, and imperfect strangers. Sometimes we inherit troubles from these imperfect people, and sometimes we create troubles all on our own. In either case, what's required is patience: patience for other people's shortcomings as well as our own.

Proverbs 16:32 teaches, "Better to be patient than powerful; better to have self-control than to conquer a city" (NLT). But for most of us, patience is difficult. We'd rather strike back than hold back. However, God has other plans. He instructs us to be patient, kind, and helpful to the people He places along our path. He instructs us to love our neighbors, even the ones who are chronically hard to live with. As believers, we must strive to obey Him, even when it's hard.

MORE FROM GOD'S WORD

But if we hope for what we do not yet have,
we wait for it patiently.
ROMANS 8:25 NIV

Be joyful in hope, patient in affliction,
faithful in prayer.
ROMANS 12:12 NIV

Patience of spirit is better than haughtiness of spirit.
ECCLESIASTES 7:8 NASB

Better to be patient than powerful; better to have
self-control than to conquer a city.
PROVERBS 16:32 NLT

The LORD is good to those who depend on him,
to those who search for him. So it is good to wait
quietly for salvation from the LORD.
LAMENTATIONS 3:25–26 NLT

MORE THOUGHTS

Frustration is not the will of God. There is time to do anything and everything that God wants us to do.
ELISABETH ELLIOT

Patience is the companion of wisdom.
SAINT AUGUSTINE

Patience graciously, compassionately, and with understanding judges the faults of others without unjust criticism.
BILLY GRAHAM

Today, take a complicated situation and with time, patience, and a smile, turn it into something positive—for you and for others.
JONI EARECKSON TADA

Some of your greatest blessings come with patience.
WARREN WIERSBE

REMEMBER THIS

God's Word teaches us to be patient, even when it's hard. God has been patient with you; now it's your turn to be patient with others. Even when it's hard.

GET PRACTICAL

When you're dealing with difficult people, it's easy to respond negatively and it's hard to be patient...hard, but not impossible. Think about ways that patience pays and impatience costs.

—⚬⚬⚬—

A CONVERSATION STARTER

Talk to a friend about the power of patience and the need to joyfully accept God's timetable.

YOUR THOUGHTS
ABOUT PATIENCE

Write down your thoughts about the rewards of patience and the potential costs of impatience.

....

....

....

....

....

....

....

....

....

....

....

14

THE QUESTION

When I encounter someone with a difficult personality, it robs me of my peace of mind. What does the Bible teach us about peace?

THE ANSWER

God's peace surpasses human understanding. When we accept His peace, it revolutionizes our lives. When we call upon Him, He can restore our souls.

Prayer guards hearts and minds and causes God to bring peace out of chaos.

BETH MOORE

STAY PEACEFUL

*Peace I leave with you, My peace I give to you;
not as the world gives do I give to you. Let not your
heart be troubled, neither let it be afraid.*
JOHN 14:27 NKJV

When you encounter a difficult person, it's up to you, and
nobody else, to maintain your peace of mind. Of course, the
other person's prickly personality may make your job harder.
After all, difficult people have a way of riling up our emotions
and distorting our thoughts. But with God's help, and with a little common sense, we can find peace amid the emotional storm.

Life is too short to allow another person's problematic personality to invade your psyche and ruin your day. But because
human emotions are contagious, there's always the danger that
you'll be drawn into the other person's mental state, with pre-
dictably negative consequences.

A far better strategy is to step back from the situation, to
say a silent prayer, and to ask God to help you retain a sense of
calm. When you do, He'll answer your prayer, the storm will
pass, and you'll be glad you retained your emotional stability,
even though the people around you were losing theirs.

MORE FROM GOD'S WORD

But the fruit of the Spirit is love, joy, peace, patience, kindness, goodness, faith, gentleness, self-control. Against such things there is no law.
GALATIANS 5:22–23 HCSB

"I will give peace, real peace, to those far and near, and I will heal them," says the LORD.
ISAIAH 57:19 NCV

He Himself is our peace.
EPHESIANS 2:14 NASB

The peace of God, which passeth all understanding, shall keep your hearts and minds through Christ Jesus.
PHILIPPIANS 4:7 KJV

These things I have spoken to you, that in Me you may have peace. In the world you will have tribulation; but be of good cheer, I have overcome the world.
JOHN 16:33 NKJV

MORE THOUGHTS

*God's power is great enough for our
deepest desperation. You can go on.
You can pick up the pieces and start anew.
You can face your fears. You can find peace
in the rubble. There is healing for your soul.*

SUZANNE DALE EZELL

*Deep within the center of the soul is a
chamber of peace where God lives and where,
if we will enter it and quiet all the other sounds,
we can hear His gentle whisper.*

LETTIE COWMAN

*Peace does not mean to be in a place
where there is no noise, trouble, or hard work.
Peace means to be in the midst of all those things
and still be calm in your heart.*

CATHERINE MARSHALL

*In the center of a hurricane there is absolute
quiet and peace. There is no safer place than
in the center of the will of God.*

CORRIE TEN BOOM

*Only Christ can meet the deepest needs
of our world and our hearts. Christ alone
can bring lasting peace.*

BILLY GRAHAM

REMEMBER THIS

God's peace is available to you this very moment if you place your absolute trust in Him. The Lord is your Shepherd. Trust Him today and be blessed.

GET PRACTICAL

God's peace can be yours if you open up your heart and invite Him in. He can restore your soul if you let Him. The rest is up to you.

—⦚—

A CONVERSATION STARTER

The Lord promises that we can experience the peace that passes all understanding. Talk to a friend about ways that both of you can discover God's peace.

YOUR THOUGHTS
ABOUT PEACE

Write down your thoughts about ways you can find peace and keep it.

....

....

....

....

....

....

....

....

....

....

....

15

THE QUESTION

When people upset me, my emotions seem to take over. What can I do to control them?

THE ANSWER

One thing you can do is to pray early and often about the people who have upset you.
It's a great way to make sure that your heart is in tune with God. The more you talk to Him, the more He will talk to you.

A feeling of real need is always a good enough reason to pray.

HANNAH WHITALL SMITH

STAY PRAYERFUL

*Rejoice always, pray without ceasing,
in everything give thanks; for this is
the will of God in Christ Jesus for you.*

1 THESSALONIANS 5:16–18 NKJV

If you're having trouble dealing with a difficult person, talk to God about it. The Lord has many important lessons to teach you, and this may be one of them. He has promised to guide you and protect you. Your task, simply put, is to listen and obey.

Perhaps, on occasion, you may find yourself overwhelmed by the challenges of everyday life. Perhaps you may forget to slow yourself down long enough to talk with God. Instead of turning your thoughts and prayers to Him, you may rely upon your own resources. Instead of asking God for guidance, you may depend only upon your own limited wisdom. A far better course of action is this: Stop what you're doing long enough to open up your heart to the Creator, and then listen carefully for His direction. In all things, great and small, seek the Lord's wisdom and His grace. He hears your prayers, and He will answer. All you must do is ask.

MORE FROM GOD'S WORD

Confess your trespasses to one another,
and pray for one another, that you may be healed.
The effective, fervent prayer of a righteous man
avails much.
JAMES 5:16 NKJV

And whenever you stand praying,
if you have anything against anyone,
forgive him, so that your Father in heaven
will also forgive you your wrongdoing.
MARK 11:25 HCSB

I desire therefore that the men pray everywhere,
lifting up holy hands, without wrath and doubting.
1 TIMOTHY 2:8 NKJV

Is anyone among you suffering? He should pray.
JAMES 5:13 HCSB

Ask, and it will be given to you; seek, and you
will find; knock, and it will be opened to you.
For everyone who asks receives, and he who seeks
finds, and to him who knocks it will be opened.
MATTHEW 7:7–8 NASB

MORE THOUGHTS

*It is impossible to overstate the need
for prayer in the fabric of family life.*

JAMES DOBSON

Prayer is our lifeline to God.

BILLY GRAHAM

*Two wings are necessary to lift our souls toward
God: prayer and praise. Prayer asks.
Praise accepts the answer.*

LETTIE COWMAN

*Don't pray when you feel like it. Have an
appointment with the Lord and keep it.*

CORRIE TEN BOOM

*Any concern that is too small to be turned into a
prayer is too small to be made into a burden.*

CORRIE TEN BOOM

REMEMBER THIS

If you're having trouble dealing with a difficult person, pray about it. Prayer changes things, and it changes you. So, pray.

GET PRACTICAL

If you're having trouble with another person, pray for that person and pray for guidance. When you ask for God's help, He'll heal your heart and guide your path.

A CONVERSATION STARTER

Talk to a friend about your experiences concerning prayer: times when your prayer life was meaningful and other times when you found it hard to pray. How did the quality and quantity of your prayers impact other aspects of your life?

YOUR THOUGHTS
ABOUT PRAYER

Write down your thoughts about the power of prayer.

....

....

....

....

....

....

....

....

....

....

....

16

THE QUESTION

Sometimes I'm tempted to gripe and complain about the difficult people in my life. What does the Bible say about complaining?

THE ANSWER

God's Word teaches us that perpetual complaining is a very bad habit. And it's contagious. So, please be sure that your friends and family members can't catch it from you!

Whenever you catch yourself starting to complain about someone, you would do well to turn your thoughts inward and inspect your own thoughts and deeds.

Saint Stephen of Muret

COMPLAINING DOESN'T HELP

Do everything without complaining or arguing.
Then you will be innocent and without any wrong.
PHILIPPIANS 2:14–15 NCV

Most of us have more blessings than we can count, yet we still find things to complain about. To complain, of course, is not only shortsighted, but it is also a serious roadblock on the path to spiritual abundance. But in our weakest moments we still grumble, whine, and moan about difficult people or the difficult circumstances they seem to create for us on a daily basis. Sometimes we give voice to our complaints, and on other occasions, we manage to keep our protests to ourselves. But even when no one else hears our complaints, God does.

Would you like to feel more comfortable about your circumstances and your life? Then promise yourself that you'll do whatever it takes to focus your thoughts and energy on the major blessings you've received, not the minor hardships— or the difficult people—you must occasionally endure.

So, the next time you're tempted to complain about the inevitable frustrations of everyday living, don't do it. Today and every day, make it a practice to count your blessings, not your inconveniences. It's the truly decent way to live.

MORE FROM GOD'S WORD

Be hospitable to one another without complaining.
1 PETER 4:9 HCSB

He who guards his lips guards his life,
but he who speaks rashly will come to ruin.
PROVERBS 13:3 NIV

A fool's displeasure is known at once,
but whoever ignores an insult is sensible.
PROVERBS 12:16 HCSB

If anyone considers himself religious and yet does
not keep a tight rein on his tongue, he deceives
himself and his religion is worthless.
JAMES 1:26 NIV

My dear brothers and sisters, always be willing
to listen and slow to speak.
JAMES 1:19 NCV

MORE THOUGHTS

*Grumbling and gratitude are, for the child of God,
in conflict. Be grateful and you won't grumble.
Grumble and you won't be grateful.*

BILLY GRAHAM

*Thanksgiving or complaining—these words
express two contrasting attitudes of the souls of
God's children. The soul that gives thanks can find
comfort in everything; the soul that complains
can find comfort in nothing.*

HANNAH WHITALL SMITH

*It is always possible to be thankful for what is given
rather than complain about what is not given.
One or the other becomes a habit of life.*

ELISABETH ELLIOT

*Don't complain. The more you complain
about things, the more things you'll
have to complain about.*

E. STANLEY JONES

*If we have our eyes upon ourselves, our problems,
and our pain, we cannot lift our eyes upward.*

BILLY GRAHAM

REMEMBER THIS

If you genuinely seek God's peace, you'll fill your heart with gratitude. When you do, there's simply no room left for complaints about difficult people, or anything else for that matter.

GET PRACTICAL

Try to keep track of the times when you complain, either to someone else or to yourself. Also, make note of the times when you express gratitude to the Lord. Do you spend more time complaining or praising?

—⁓—

A CONVERSATION STARTER

Talk to a friend about the emotional and spiritual costs associated with constant complaining. And if you complain more than you should, talk about ways that you can shutter your personal complaint factory for good.

YOUR THOUGHTS
ABOUT COMPLAINING

List ways in which you can complain less and do more.

....

....

....

....

....

....

....

....

....

....

....

17

THE QUESTION

It's hard for me to forgive the people who have hurt me. What does the Bible say about that?

THE ANSWER

God's Word instructs you to forgive others—no exceptions. Forgiveness is its own reward and bitterness is its own punishment, so guard your words and your thoughts accordingly.

He who cannot forgive others breaks the bridge over which he himself must pass.

CORRIE TEN BOOM

FORGIVENESS NOW

And whenever you stand praying,
if you have anything against anyone, forgive him,
so that your Father in heaven will also
forgive you your wrongdoing.

MARK 11:25 HCSB

Difficult people can be hard to forgive, but forgive them we must. To do otherwise is to disobey our Father in heaven.

When you make the choice to forgive, when you genuinely let go of all anger and resentment, you'll feel better about yourself and your world. Why? Because God grants peace to those who honor Him by obeying His commandments and following in the footsteps of His Son.

The familiar words of John 14:27 remind us that Christ offers us peace, not as the world gives, but as He alone gives: "Peace I leave with you. My peace I give to you. I do not give to you as the world gives. Your heart must not be troubled or fearful" (HCSB). Have you discovered that peace? Or are you still rushing after the artificial brand of "peace and contentment" that the world promises but cannot deliver?

Today, as a gift to yourself and to your loved ones, forgive everyone who has ever harmed you. Then claim the inner peace that is your spiritual birthright: the peace of Jesus Christ. It is always available; it has been paid for in full; it is yours for the asking. So ask, receive, and share.

MORE FROM GOD'S WORD

*And be kind to one another, tenderhearted,
forgiving one another, even as God in Christ
forgave you.*

Ephesians 4:32 NKJV

*Judge not, and you shall not be judged.
Condemn not, and you shall not be condemned.
Forgive, and you will be forgiven.*

Luke 6:37 NKJV

*Above all, love each other deeply, because love
covers over a multitude of sins.*

1 Peter 4:8 NIV

*But I say to you, love your enemies and pray
for those who persecute you.*

Matthew 5:44 NASB

*The merciful are blesssed,
for they will be shown mercy.*

Matthew 5:7 HCSB

MORE THOUGHTS

Forgiveness is God's command.
MARTIN LUTHER

*Forgiveness does not change the past,
but it does enlarge the future.*
DAVID JEREMIAH

*One bold stroke, forgiveness obliterates the past
and permits us to enter the land of new beginnings.*
BILLY GRAHAM

*Forgiveness is an act of the will, and the will can
function regardless of the temperature of the heart.*
CORRIE TEN BOOM

*Forgiveness is one of the most beautiful words in
the human vocabulary. How much pain could be
avoided if we all learned the meaning of this word!*
BILLY GRAHAM

REMEMBER THIS

God commands us to love all people, regardless of their personality styles. So, don't be quick to judge others. Instead, be quick to forgive them.

GET PRACTICAL

Make a list of the people whom you still need to forgive. Then ask God to cleanse your heart of bitterness, animosity, and regret. If you ask Him sincerely and often, He will respond.

A CONVERSATION STARTER

Talk to a friend about the rewards of forgiving and the costs of not forgiving.

YOUR THOUGHTS
ABOUT FORGIVENESS

List the people whom you need to forgive today. Then pray about those people on your list.

....

....

....

....

....

....

....

....

....

....

18

THE QUESTION

Why is it important for me to overcome
feelings of bitterness?

THE ANSWER

Until you can forgive others, you'll be trapped in
an emotional prison of your own making.

*Resentment always hurts you more
than the person you resent.*

RICK WARREN

BITTERNESS:
BEWARE OF THE POISON

He who says he is in the light, and hates his brother,
is in darkness until now.

1 JOHN 2:9 NKJV

Bitterness is a spiritual sickness. It will consume your soul; it is dangerous to your emotional health; it can destroy you if you let it. So, don't let it!

The world holds few if any rewards for those who remain angrily focused upon the past. Still, the act of forgiveness is difficult for all but the most saintly men and women. Being frail, fallible, imperfect human beings, most of us are quick to anger, quick to blame, slow to forgive, and even slower to forget. Yet we know that it's best to forgive others, just as we, too, have been forgiven.

If there exists even one person—including yourself—against whom you still harbor bitter feelings, it's time to forgive and move on. Bitterness and regret are not part of God's plan for your life, but God won't force you to forgive others. It's a job that only you can finish, and the sooner you finish it, the better.

If you are caught up in intense feelings of anger or resentment, you know all too well the destructive power of these emotions. How can you rid yourself of these feelings? First, you must prayerfully ask God to cleanse your heart. Then you must learn to catch yourself whenever thoughts of bitterness or hatred begin to attack you. Your challenge is this: You must learn to resist negative thoughts before they hijack your emotions. When you learn to direct your thoughts toward more positive topics, you'll be protected from the spiritual and emotional consequences of bitterness...and you'll be wiser, healthier, and happier, too.

MORE FROM GOD'S WORD

You have heard that it was said,
"Love your neighbor and hate your enemy."
But I tell you: Love your enemies and pray
for those who persecute you, that you may be
sons of your Father in heaven.
MATTHEW 5:43–45 NIV

My dear brothers and sisters, always be willing to
listen and slow to speak. Do not become
angry easily, because anger will not help you
live the right kind of life God wants.
JAMES 1:19–20 NCV

If anyone claims, "I am living in the light,"
but hates a fellow believer,
that person is still living in darkness.
1 JOHN 2:9 NLT

Everyone must be quick to hear, slow to speak,
and slow to anger, for man's anger does not
accomplish God's righteousness.
JAMES 1:19–20 HCSB

Do not be conquered by evil,
but conquer evil with good.
ROMANS 12:21 HCSB

MORE THOUGHTS

*He who cannot forgive others breaks the bridge
over which he himself must pass.*

CORRIE TEN BOOM

*Bitterness is a spiritual cancer, a rapidly growing
malignancy that can consume your life. Bitterness
cannot be ignored, but [it] must be healed at the
very core, and only Christ can heal bitterness.*

BETH MOORE

Bitterness imprisons life; love releases it.

HARRY EMERSON FOSDICK

*Bitterness is anger gone sour, an attitude
of deep discontent that poisons our souls
and destroys our peace.*

BILLY GRAHAM

*Revenge easily descends into an endless
cycle of hate and violence. The Bible says
to never repay evil with evil.*

BILLY GRAHAM

REMEMBER THIS

The Bible warns that bitterness is both dangerous and self-destructive. So today, make a list of the people whom you need to forgive and the things that you need to forget. Then ask God to give you the strength to forgive and move on.

GET PRACTICAL

You can never fully enjoy the present if you're bitter about the past. So, instead of living in the past, make peace with it and move on.

A CONVERSATION STARTER

Talk to a friend about an event in your past that still disturbs you. Then discuss any ways in which you could begin to make peace with your past and move on.

YOUR THOUGHTS
ABOUT THE PAST

List the things you can do to make peace with your past and move beyond any current bitter feelings.

19

THE QUESTION

Peer pressure is everywhere, and some people are constantly encouraging me to do things I don't believe are right. What should I do?

THE ANSWER

The world is full of temptations, and some people will encourage you to give in to them. Because you can't please everybody, you're better off simply trying to please God.

Friend, don't go along with evil. Model the good. The person who does good does God's work. The person who does evil falsifies God, doesn't know the first thing about God.

3 John 1:11 MSG

DON'T COMPROMISE YOURSELF

Let integrity and uprightness preserve me,
for I wait for You.
PSALM 25:21 NKJV

Sometimes difficult people encourage us to behave immaturely, or unethically, or both. On these occasions, we may be tempted to focus on external forces and persuasive personalities, not on the conscience that God has placed deep within our hearts. But if we disregard that quiet inner voice, we make a profound mistake.

Integrity is built slowly over a lifetime. It is a precious thing—difficult to build but easy to tear down. As believers in Christ, we must seek to live each day with discipline, honesty, and faith. When we do, at least two things will take place: integrity will become a habit, and God will bless us because of our obedience to Him.

Would you like a time-tested formula for successful living? Here is a simple one that is proven and true: Don't compromise yourself. Period.

Instead of getting lost in the crowd, seek guidance from God. Instead of giving in to the unreasonable demands of a difficult person, stand your ground. Instead of tuning out your conscience, tune in to it. Does this sound too simplistic? Perhaps it is simple, but it is also the only way to reap all the marvelous riches that God has in store for you.

MORE FROM GOD'S WORD

He stores up success for the upright; He is a shield for those who live with integrity.
PROVERBS 2:7 HCSB

The godly walk with integrity; blessed are their children who follow them.
PROVERBS 20:7 NLT

The integrity of the upright guides them, but the perversity of the treacherous destroys them.
PROVERBS 11:3 HCSB

The godly are directed by honesty.
PROVERBS 11:5 NLT

The man of integrity walks securely, but he who takes crooked paths will be found out.
PROVERBS 10:9 NIV

MORE THOUGHTS

Remember that your character
is the sum total of your habits.
RICK WARREN

True greatness is not measured by headlines
or wealth. The inner character of a person
is the true measure of lasting greatness.
BILLY GRAHAM

Character is what you are in the dark.
D. L. MOODY

Character is built over a lifetime.
ELIZABETH GEORGE

Let your words be the genuine
picture of your heart.
JOHN WESLEY

REMEMBER THIS

God rewards integrity just as surely as He punishes duplicity. Never allow another person to bully you into doing something of which God disapproves.

GET PRACTICAL

Don't compromise yourself. If you're being bullied by a person with a difficult personality, you must summon the courage to stand up for your beliefs. When you pray for the strength to stand up for your convictions, God will help you do the right thing.

————

A CONVERSATION STARTER

Ask a friend which is more important: integrity or popularity. Discuss the possible costs of compromising your integrity for short-term personal gain or for fleeting popularity.

YOUR THOUGHTS
ABOUT INTEGRITY

Write down your thoughts about the importance of maintaining your integrity.

....

....

....

....

....

....

....

....

....

....

20

THE QUESTION

If I want God to guide me, what should I do?

THE ANSWER

When it comes to the art of dealing with difficult people, or anything else for that matter, God's Word is the final word. If you want God's guidance, ask for it. When you pray for guidance, God will give it.

—∿—

Keep asking, and it will be given to you. Keep searching, and you will find. Keep knocking, and the door will be opened to you. For everyone who asks receives, and the one who searches finds, and to the one who knocks, the door will be opened.

MATTHEW 7:7–8 HCSB

LET GOD BE YOUR GUIDE

Trust in the LORD with all your heart, and lean not on your own understanding; in all your ways acknowledge Him, and He shall direct your paths.

PROVERBS 3:5–6 NKJV

When you find yourself caught up in an emotionally charged situation, ask God for guidance. Otherwise, you may find yourself caught up in an emotional outburst that can result in bitter consequences.

God does not reward undisciplined behavior, nor does He endorse impulsive outbursts. Instead, He instructs us to be mature, thoughtful, peaceful, and patient. Yet these qualities may not come naturally for most of us, so we need His help. When we petition Him in prayer, sincerely and often, He helps us reel in our negative emotions, which, if left unchecked, will rob us of happiness and peace.

When we ask for God's guidance, with our hearts and minds open to His direction, He will lead us along a path of His choosing. But for many of us, listening to God is hard. We have so many things we want, and so many needs to pray for, that we spend far more time talking at God than we do listening to Him.

Corrie ten Boom observed, "God's guidance is even more important than common sense. I can declare that the deepest darkness is outshone by the light of Jesus." These words remind us that life is best lived when we seek the Lord's direction early and often.

Our Father has many ways to make Himself known. Our challenge is to keep our spirits open to His instruction. So, if you're unsure of your next step, trust God's promises and spend time often in His presence. When you do, He'll guide your steps today, tomorrow, and forever.

MORE FROM GOD'S WORD

Teach me to do Your will, for You are my God; Your Spirit is good. Lead me in the land of uprightness.
PSALM 143:10 NKJV

*Shew me thy ways, O LORD; teach me thy paths.
Lead me in thy truth, and teach me:
for thou art the God of my salvation;
on thee do I wait all the day.*
PSALM 25:4–5 KJV

*Yet LORD, You are our Father; we are the clay,
and You are our potter; we all are
the work of Your hands.*
ISAIAH 64:8 HCSB

*The LORD says, "I will guide you along
the best pathway for your life. I will advise you
and watch over you."*
PSALM 32:8 NLT

*Morning by morning he wakens me and opens
my understanding to his will. The Sovereign LORD
has spoken to me, and I have listened.*
ISAIAH 50:4–5 NLT

MORE THOUGHTS

*The will of God will never take us where
the grace of God cannot sustain us.*

BILLY GRAHAM

*God never leads us to do anything
that is contrary to the Bible.*

BILLY GRAHAM

*When we are obedient, God guides
our steps and our stops.*

CORRIE TEN BOOM

*Are you serious about wanting God's guidance to
become a personal reality in your life? The first step
is to tell God that you know you can't manage
your own life; that you need His help.*

CATHERINE MARSHALL

*As you walk through the valley of the unknown,
you will find the footprints of Jesus both
in front of you and beside you.*

CHARLES STANLEY

REMEMBER THIS

When you form a genuine partnership with God, you can do amazing things. So, make God your partner in every aspect of your life, including the way you manage your relationships with difficult people.

GET PRACTICAL

If you want God's guidance, ask for it. When you pray for guidance, the Lord will give it. He will guide your steps if you let Him. So let Him.

—⁓—

A CONVERSATION STARTER

Talk to a friend about specific ways in which you can learn to better hear God's voice and follow His path.

YOUR THOUGHTS
ABOUT GOD'S GUIDANCE

Write down your thoughts about the direction that God is leading you today.